3-6

FOLLOW IT!
LEARN ABOUT SHADOWS

BY PAMELA HALL

The Child's World®

Published by The Child's World®
1980 Lookout Drive • Mankato, MN 56003-1705
800-599-READ • www.childsworld.com

ACKNOWLEDGMENTS
The Child's World®: Mary Berendes, Publishing Director
Content Consultant: Paul Ohmann, PhD, Associate Professor of Physics,
    University of St. Thomas
The Design Lab: Design and production
Red Line Editorial: Editorial direction

PHOTO CREDITS: Konstantin Brednikov/iStockphoto, cover, 1, 2, 3, 4, 6,
8, 10, 12, 14, 16, 18, 20, 22; Fotolia, 5 (top), 7 (bottom), 13, 15; Michal
Slichta/Fotolia, 5 (bottom); Pavel Losevsky/Fotolia, 7 (top); Galina Barskaya/
Fotolia, 9; Tan Kian Khoon/Fotolia, 11; Danish Khan/iStockphoto, 17;
Radu Razvan/Fotolia, 19; Matthew Rambo/iStockphoto, 20; John Cairns/
iStockphoto, 21; Jane Yamada, 23

LIBRARY OF CONGRESS CATALOGING-IN-PUBLICATION DATA
Hall, Pamela.
  Follow it! Learn about shadows / by Pamela Hall ; illustrated by Jane Yamada.
    p. cm.
  ISBN 978-1-60253-508-4 (lib. bd. : alk. paper)
  1. Shades and shadows—Juvenile literature. I. Yamada, Jane, ill. II. Title.
  QC381.6.H35 2010
  535'.4—dc22   2010010975

Printed in the United States of America in Mankato, Minnesota.
July 2010
F11538

CONTENTS

Shadows Big and Small

They stretch.

They shift.

They flutter and sway.

Big and small,
shadows are everywhere.

Tall buildings cast shadows. ▶

Tiny bugs cast shadows, too. ▶

4

5

Creating Shadows

On sunny days your shadow follows you around.

But on cloudy days, you're on your own.

Why?

It takes bright light to make a shadow.

The sun helps make your shadow. ▶

When the sun is hidden, you have no shadow. ▶

Rays of light move in straight lines.

Your body blocks light's path.

Your body makes a dark shape
on the ground—a you-shaped shadow!

The bicycle blocks light rays. It makes a bicycle-shaped shadow. ▶

Ants, skyscrapers, leaves, airplanes—
most things make shadows.

These things block light.

They are **opaque**.

But some things let light shine through.

Clear glass is see-through.

It doesn't make shadows.

Glass in a window doesn't make a shadow. But the frames in a window do. ▶

Big and Bigger Shadows

On a summer day, it feels so good
to cool off in the shade.

What things make shade?
Trees, buildings, and mountains can.
Shade is just big shadows.

An umbrella
at the beach
makes shade. ▶

12

Night is an even bigger shadow.

Earth is always spinning.

During the day, your side of Earth is facing the sun.

At night, your side of Earth is away from the sun.

You are in Earth's shadow.

It's night in the parts of Earth that are in shadow. ▶

Changing Shadows

Your shadow changes throughout the day.

At noon, the sun is high in the sky. Your shadow is short.

What time of day does this picture show? ▶

16

In the morning and the evening, the sun is low.

Your shadow stretches long.

When the sun is rising or setting, your shadow is long. ▶

Where is your shadow?
It depends.

When light is in front of you,
your shadow falls behind.

But when light shines
at your back,
your shadow goes
before you.

When light is
behind you,
your shadow
is in front
of you. ▶

Where is light
coming from in
this picture? ◀

Shadow Play

It's time to play with shadows!

Can you make a shadow monster
with your hand?

Can you fit inside
your friend's shadow shape?

Make your shadow high-five
your friend's shadow.

Notice all the different
shadows around you.

Kinds of Shadows

PALE SHADOWS	BIG SHADOWS	FUZZY SHADOWS
Some things don't block out all the light. They let some light through. They make pale shadows.	Big things make big shadows. But small things can make big shadows, too. The closer something is to the light, the bigger its shadow.	When something is far away from its shadow, its shadow is fuzzy.

Words to Know

cast (KAST): To cast is to make, especially when it comes to shadows. On sunny days, your body casts a shadow.

opaque (o-PAYK): Opaque things are not see-through. By blocking light, opaque objects make shadows.

rays (RAYZ): Rays are straight lines by which light seems to travel. Shadows are made when things block light rays.